# STEAM LOCOMOTIVES

## TRAINS

Lynn M. Stone

The Rourke Corporation, Inc.
Vero Beach, Florida 32964

PHOTO CREDITS:
Cover, p. 4, 21 © Don Hennen; title page, p. 12 courtesy of Union Pacific Railroad Museum Collection; p. 7, 10, 13, 18 from the George H. Drury Collection; p. 17 © Robert Hayden; p. 8, 15 © Jerry Hennen

PRODUCED BY:
East Coast Studios, Merritt Island, Florida

EDITORIAL SERVICES:
Penworthy Learning Systems

**Library of Congress Cataloging-in-Publication Data**

Stone, Lynn M.
   Steam locomotives / by Lynn M. Stone
     p.  cm. — (Trains)
   Summary: Describes the history and uses of steam locomotives, the different types, and some famous models.
   ISBN 0-86593-520-3
   1. Steam locomotives Juvenile literature. [1. Locomotives. 2. Railroads—Trains.] I. Title. II. Series: Stone, Lynn M.  Trains.
TJ605.5.S76  1999
625.26'1—dc21
                                       99-13278
                                         CIP

**Printed in the USA**

# TABLE OF CONTENTS

## STEAM LOCOMOTIVES

For more than 100 years, steam **locomotives** (LO kuh MO tivz) ruled America's rails. Steam engines grumbled, hissed, and chugged. They puffed great clouds of smoke and steam. Sometimes they spit fiery sparks, called **cinders** (SIN derz), from their smokestacks.

Growling and thundering, steam locomotives hauled freight and passenger cars over thousands of miles of track. The steam locomotives had taken over the job of horses. They were truly iron horses.

*Steam trains with their loud whistles, black smoke, and thunder were part of America's cities and countryside for more than 100 years.*

## EARLY STEAM LOCOMOTIVES

The first steam engine that worked fairly well was built in England by Richard Trevithick in 1804. Then, 25 years later, George Stephenson, another Englishman, built a much better steam engine. And by 1830, a steam locomotive was puffing along six miles of track in South Carolina.

*This steam locomotive, built in the 1880s, was the 4-4-0, or American, type.*

## STEAM POWER AT WORK

Steam engines burn oil or coal in the locomotive's **firebox** (FIER BAHKS). The fuel is carried in the **tender** (TEN der), or coal car.

The tremendous heat of the burning fuel changes water in the locomotive's boiler to steam. Steam is forced into the engine. Pressure from the steam moves steel rods attached to the locomotive's driving wheels. As heat increases, pressure builds and the wheels go faster.

*Steam locomotives carried fuel in a tender, or "coal car." While this locomotive burned coal, many locomotives on Western railroads burned oil.*

# LOCOMOTIVE WHEELS

Driving wheels are the large wheels that have the power to move a locomotive and its train. Most steam locomotives also have smaller wheels in front and in back of the driving wheels.

The small wheels in their groups are called **trucks** (TRUKZ). The groups of wheels under train cars are also called "trucks."

The front truck helps guide a locomotive into curves. The rear truck helps hold the weight of the firebox.

*Mechanics work on a steam locomotive. The driving wheel (left) is taller than the man next to it.*

*A 4-8-8-4 Union Pacific Railroad Big Boy steams through Colorado in September, 1942, early in World War II.*

*In 1944, a Boston and Maine steam train waited at North Station in Boston. Steam locomotives still ruled America's rails during World War II (1941-1945).*

A locomotive's wheels, large and small, help identify it. A locomotive called a 4-8-2, for example, has four small wheels on its front truck, two on each side. It has eight driving wheels, four on each side. It has two wheels, one on each side, on its rear truck.

The 4-8-2 locomotives were the most popular American steam units. The largest American steam engines, though, were Union Pacific's 4-8-8-4 Big Boys of the 1940s. Big Boys had two groups of driving wheels.

*A 4-6-0 ten-wheeler rests by a wooden water tower. Steam engines needed plenty of water for their boilers.*

# FAMOUS STEAM LOCOMOTIVES

Well-known steam engines were often named for the places where they were first used. The common 4-8-2's were known as the Mountain type. They were especially popular in the mountains of the East. The 4-8-4 locomotives were called the Northern type. Among others were those known as the Pacifics (4-6-2), Atlantics (4-4-2), Berkshires (2-8-4), and Prairies (2-6-2).

*Rio Grande's 2-8-2, a Mikado type locomotive, steams across Colorado plains.*

## STREAMLINED STEAM LOCOMOTIVES

In the mid-1930s, many railroads began to streamline some of their steam locomotives. These locomotives were given new steel covers.

Streamlining didn't change how the locomotive worked. Under the new cover was still a steam locomotive. But streamlining made the locomotives look more modern.

The first of these streamlined locomotives was the New York Central Railroad's *Commodore Vanderbilt.*

*The Southern Pacific Railroad began using streamlined locomotives in the 1930s. By the late 1940s, most of the sleek steamers had been replaced by diesel locomotives.*

# THE END OF STEAM POWER

Steam locomotives were built in the United States as late as 1950. But American steam power, even by the late 1930s, had no future.

In 1929 American railroads had nearly 60,000 steam locomotives. Diesel-electric locomotives were almost unknown, but that would soon change.

Fast, powerful diesel-electrics began to appear in the 1930s. They were cheaper to run than steam locomotives. And diesels didn't need nearly as much repair and service as steam locomotives. Railroading without steam engines would never be the same.

*The Mid-Continent Railway Museum in North Freedom, Wisconsin, is one of several places where you can still see—and ride—steam trains.*

One by one, the railroads gave up their steam locomotives and replaced them with diesels. Between 1944 and 1955, the number of steam locomotives dropped from about 40,000 to under 6,000. Meanwhile, nearly 25,000 diesels were on the rails.

By 1960, just 261 steam locomotives were in regular service on American railroads. They would soon disappear, too.

Several steam locomotives have been saved from the scrap heap. On special days, these old iron horses are brought out. Once again, tourists can relive the old days of railroad smoke and thunder.

# GLOSSARY

**cinder** (SIN der) — bits of burned or burning coal that rises out of a steam locomotive's smoke stack

**firebox** (FIER BAHKS) — part of a steam locomotive where the fuel is burned, usually behind the boiler, in the cab

**locomotive** (LO kuh MO tiv) — a power plant or engine on wheels used to push or pull railroad cars; a train engine

**tender** (TEN der) — a car that carries fuel and water, placed directly behind a steam locomotive; a "coal car"

**truck** (TRUK) — any set of wheels under train cars or under a locomotive

# INDEX

# FURTHER READING

Find out more about trains with these helpful books and information sites:
Riley, C.J. *The Encyclopedia of Trains and Locomotives.* Metro Books, 1995

Association of American Railroads online at www.aar.org
California State Railroad Museum online at www.csrmf.org
Union Pacific Railroad online at http://www.uprr.com